T0086717

Questions and
Their Retinue

البحث عن جدتي

هذا الغطاءُ، هذه الرياشُ والأصابعُ الذهبُ
تلك العصا
وسحرها، ومنطُ عربها الخشبُ
وذلك الإبريقُ صامتاً، وأزرقاً أراهُ .
هذا الغبارُ المملكه
أنفضه
برنزٌ كالرّماد
رأيتُها
تنفّتت
تمايلتْ إلى أمامْ
تمايلتْ إلى وراءْ
وانفجرتْ بأنّةٍ !
همستُ: جدتي
صرختُ: جدتي
أخذتُ، زمجرتُ
ودفعةٌ واحدةٌ
صارت هباءْ

Questions and Their Retinue

Selected Poems of Hatif Janabi

Translated from the Arabic
and with an Introduction
by Khaled Mattawa

The University of Arkansas Press
Fayetteville   1996

Copyright 1996 by the University of Arkansas Board of Trustees

All rights reserved
Manufactured in the United States of America

00   99   98   97   96   5   4   3   2   1

Designed by Liz Lester

☉ The paper used in this publication meets the minimum requirements of the American National Standard for Permanence of Paper for Printed Library Materials Z39.48-1984.

Library of Congress Cataloging-in-Publication Data

Janabi, Hatif, 1952–
        [Poems. English. Selections]
        Questions and their retinue / selected poems of Hatif Janabi; translated from the Arabic and with an introduction by Khaled Mattawa.
            p.   cm.
        ISBN 1-55728-431-8 (alk. paper). —ISBN 1-55728-432-6 (pbk. : alk. paper)
        1. Janabi, Hatif, 1952– —Translations into English.
        I. Mattawa, Khaled. II. Title.
        PJ7840.A49A24   1996
        892' .716—dc20   96–12896
                                                             CIP

For my mother

—H. J.

Acknowledgments

Thanks to the editors of the following magazines in which the English translations of some of these poems were originally published, in slightly different form: *Indiana Review, Connecticut Review, Artful Dodge, Graham House Review, Kaleidoscope, Breeze, Tampa Review,* and *International Quarterly.*

Many, many thanks to Professor Salih Al-Toma for reviewing the accuracy of the translation and for giving continuous and generous support to this project; to Jennifer Grotz, Chris Green, and Adam Sol for reviewing the clarity and flow of the English text and for their insightful and cheerful companionship; and to Professor Adnan Haydar for his helpful remarks.

Contents

Introduction

The first time I read Hatif Janabi's poems was in September 1993 while he was a visiting scholar at Indiana University. It was his first week in America, and we were having lunch at a garden restaurant on a beautiful day in Bloomington. As I read the poems, I sensed how widely they differed from the scene in which we were meeting. The poems were passionate and jolting and could not be read without serious attention. They were not poems that would blend in with one's environment; rather, they demanded that the reader transplant himself in them. I took them home having decided to translate them.

Even though I had been following contemporary Arabic poetry closely, I had not read until then anyone who sounded like Hatif Janabi. Yes, the poems were aggrieved—and what else should one expect from a poet fleeing a brutal political regime?—but they were ingenuous in the way they shifted moods. The speaker in many of Janabi's poems resembled John Berryman's Henry in "Dream Songs"; the speaker moved from a macho confrontational stance to resigned desperation, and from coyness to a deep longing where sometimes hope crept in. The associative processes and the sometimes bizarre surreal imagery Janabi employed were very effective in expressing his profound sense of political and spiritual alienation. I liked how his poems combined humor, mostly of a farcical type, with passionate earnest pleas for human compassion and understanding.

The mood shifts the poems took were matched by shifts in cadence. Sprawled all over the page, the poems seemed to gesticulate wildly at times. Other poems seemed subdued and pensive. They had arcane punctuation and eccentric numerical divisions as if to frustrate any attempt to render them logical. The poems were, in Auden's words, "clear expressions of mixed feelings."

Of course, Auden's axiom may have encouraged many a poet to write vaguely rather than to write clearly about ambiguous or difficult subjects. In Janabi's poems, surreal images, stark and absorbing, help the reader have something to visualize continuously even if the direction that the poem is taking is unclear. In this way Janabi's poems are cinematic in the best sense of the word. They always require rereading, and each rereading is a visitation of the work of a brilliant visualizer.

Hatif Janabi was born in 1952 in Ghammas, Iraq, near Kadissia, site of the historic battle that facilitated the Arab conquest of Iraq and Persia in the seventh century. His father, a merchant landowner, pursued a lifelong interest in law and jurisprudence; his mother, a homemaker, memorized a great deal of folk poetry and sang it to her children and relatives. Janabi attributes to his mother his love of poetry and his fascination with rhythm as a spiritual force. Both parents were illiterate. In 1963 a murder in Janabi's village led to a prolonged conflict in which his family became embroiled. One of the farm workers employed by Janabi's father was the murderer, which ostensibly meant that anyone related to the culprit was a potential target. His father left the village hoping that the conflict would eventually die out. One night, however, the murdered man's family threatened the Janabi household. Janabi recounts how his mother smuggled him late that night to a boat that sailed him to safety on the other bank of the Euphrates. The family eventually reunited in Baghdad where they spent a few months with relatives, then went on to Najaf, a Shiite holy city, where his father attempted to reestablish business connections. The family never returned to Ghammas, their previous economic comfort was never recovered, and, as Janabi says, it was his first encounter with exile.

Najaf, with its various Shiite festivals and rituals, was a fascinating place for Janabi. The Shiites, though a large minority in Iraq, have been for centuries an oppressed group. Their highly exhibitionistic rituals, particularly the parades to commemorate Hussain's martyrdom in which men engage in self-flagellation, made a great impression on Janabi. There he sensed "man's inclination to adopt a tragic stance of his condition" and he learned to distrust that "trap." The participants in these rituals commemorated an assassination that occurred fourteen hundred years earlier and reveled in a deep sense of tragedy that ultimately led to a kind of euphoria. Janabi came to believe that "man is prey to exaggeration in everything, and he is the only creature who builds traps for himself and is proud to have done so." I think the parades were educational to him as insights into extreme forms of expression, insights that he put to good use in his poetry. Janabi continued to watch Shiite rituals—they are hard to ignore in Najaf—but also developed an interest in astronomy and reading. The books finally won out over the stars, and he became an avid reader. His readings included pre-Islamic poetry, the Bible, the epic of Gilgamesh, Sufi poetry, Dante, Rumi, Cervantes, Dostoevsky, and Kafka. Hatif tells a story of reading books by Freud and Marx and other "bearded" authors; his father once warned him that reading books by "the father of the beard" (whatever his political affiliation might be) would only lead him into trouble. At the age of fifteen Janabi began to write poems.

Upon completing high school in 1968, Janabi entered Baghdad University to study Arabic literature after his father refused to allow him to enroll in the College of Fine Arts where he hoped to pursue painting. To support himself in college, he sold cigarettes outside movie houses. Occasionally, he sold women's underwear as a way to meet women. In Baghdad he became more acquainted with the literary figures there and began to develop a reputation as an original young poet. His difficult economic situation and the hegemony of leftist thought on the Iraqi cultural scene raised in Janabi the wish to pursue his writing elsewhere.

After college he was conscripted in the military and served a difficult year in the marshlands of southern Iraq. Then he was given a teaching post in Kirkuk, hundreds of miles from his family in Baghdad. Kirkuk was a learning experience for Janabi. A multi-racial, multireligious city made up of Arabs, Persians, Kurds, Turkoman, and adherents of Islam, Christianity, Judaism, and Zoroastrianism, Kirkuk educated him about coexistence and the necessity for intercultural dialogue. After living there for three years, Janabi felt he could live anywhere in the world. When the Iraqi government began a bloody campaign against its critics in 1976, he decided it was time to breathe "a different air."

In 1976, his passport stamped with visas to six Eastern European countries, Janabi, carrying a few hundred dollars, boarded a bus heading northwest. He took the bus in order to avoid the Baghdad airport and its dangerous interrogators. He had obtained a scholarship from the Polish government to study there. The trip took him across Turkey, Bulgaria, and Rumania. At a Soviet checkpoint, where he had hoped to cross into Poland, he was refused entry. He turned back into Rumania, taking a different route to Poland. Arriving in Krakow to study Polish, he was not sure he wanted to stay at first. He had hopes of crossing into Germany and on to the West. But his difficult trip, which had taken several weeks, and the warmth with which he was met in Poland convinced him to stay.

And in Poland he stayed, earning a master's in Polish literature and a doctorate in drama from Warsaw University. It might be ironic to say that Janabi felt freedom for the first time in communist Poland, but it is true. As an exile writing in a foreign language, he did not have to face the censorship that Polish authors did, and he wrote whatever he wanted. Socially, the atmosphere in Poland was liberating in comparison to the repression he felt during his youth in Iraq. He traveled in Eastern Europe, partied with friends, met women, fell in love—these were the pleasures of freedom he had not experienced earlier. After ten years in Poland, and particularly during the difficult Solidarity years, Janabi felt it was time to reconnect himself with the Arab world. In 1987 he traveled to Algeria to teach as a lecturer at Tizi Ouzou University. The contact was fruitful. It gave him a new landscape and new challenges. He wrote a great deal there. But the Algerian government's treatment of Arab expatriates on its territory finally drove him out. In 1990 he resettled in Poland to teach at Warsaw University and became a Polish citizen the following year.

Janabi is among a generation of Arab poets who, because of censorship, could speak only obliquely about the reality of their environment. In their poems they created symbolic, surreal landscapes that attempted to reveal the political and psychological stresses under which people lived. This was a survival technique, similar to those adopted by Eastern European poets who reverted to ancient history and mythology to address the ills of the Soviet Bloc. We see an example of Janabi's use of the symbolic landscape in his early poems such as "Playing the Skull." The poem does not contain a single reference to Iraq. It does not occur in a real place or even in real time. The poem seeks a visualization of the psychic landscape in which individuals reside.

"Playing the Skull" is a nightmare soliloquy. We are told about a kind of nightmare, but it is occurring as we are told about it. The speaker is both narrator and actor. In his daily life the speaker tells us:

> God was a loaf of bread I chased
> in the morning
> and in secret I fixed my eyes the devil's way.

Around him poverty flows "in torrents." The speaker flogs his love, burns his passions, his dreams "a circle, / red chains and white." The world haunts him with a vision of himself becoming

> a spear leaved with miracle-dreams and skeletons
> and a weeping woman
> and a laughing woman.

No one can help him as "Each huddles by the window of his miseries and weeps." Being in such a state, where patience is no solution because it too weeps, the speaker longs for an end to things as they stand: "I long for the nerves of the universe to crack, / I long to bury my face in a greater rage." He vows:

> I will flee my skull,
> I will draw imaginary steps between the dead and the living,
> I will hang my skull from children's belts.

As a reaction to his situation, the first line may be understandable; the speaker simply wants to escape his condition. It is not a wish for death, however, but a wish to be somewhere between life and death. In this position he hopes to connect the living with the dead by drawing imaginary steps between them. And as his skull hangs from children's belts, he hopes to affirm the notion that there is no future—only a state of living that resembles death, a state in which the speaker finds his people and himself. Wishing to be without a skull, to be living-dead, is reflective of the speaker's desire to live without illusion.

In the two stanzas that follow, the nightmare unfolds. The wall that wound around the speaker leaves him, and he crosses to the other bank. There he encounters the Pharaoh and his army. In this nightmare the speaker finds an opportunity for heroism. The world offers him poison to drink and he refuses. Because the verb is "offer," "poison" has to be read as a metaphor. The world is not forcing the speaker to drink the poison; it is merely offering it. Hence, the "poison" could be propaganda, a bribe, anything that would poison the speaker's being. Nonetheless, he refuses, and the horror begins. The speaker starts to actively pursue an end to it. He tries to appease the Pharaoh, calling him "a friend" and "my love." He offers his heart as a plate. He tells someone, "Do not despair." He gathers the people around him. But at the end of this nightmare the only thing he can do is "comfort the shocked ones with patience." The speaker knows this does not work because comforting the shocked ones with patience is exactly what happened in the real world. The nightmare, therefore, has to end. It was going to provide the speaker with his only opportunity for heroism, but there, too, the forces of evil proved insurmountable.

In the last two stanzas the speaker returns to his reality. He asks for someone to rescue his nation with a chair "to rest in during its comatose hours" and a hearse for it "to spend its old age in." This is not what he is willing to do, however. The speaker is vital and alive "like a cloud raining patience / raining longing and tenderness." In the last stanza he disintegrates into rain where he is befriended with streams and tears. The last line of the poem indicates that the speaker is not finished. He has not told us everything as "only a lover knows [his] secret." The potential for heroism is reinstated, and we sense he has not surrendered yet.

"Playing the Skull" was written in Iraq in 1972. It is possible to argue that Janabi's explorations of the image and of surrealism in this poem were merely practical solutions to evade the censor. In fact, they were not; rather, they were aesthetic choices to which he was committed. In doing so Janabi suggests that regimes and institutions do battle for the imagination of an individual—it is important to them that imagination be limited. We are made aware that real freedom, if we were to seek it, is a difficult road filled, as Janabi demonstrates, with merciless iron hands, crippling fears, and, ultimately, a sense of hopelessness. In these poems we see the struggle with demons, with the border crossings that guard their genitals with iron bars, with spies crouching on the road, as well as with melancholy and disillusionment.

Janabi's exile to Poland alleviated many of his immediate concerns, but he saw exile not as a solution but rather as an extension of the power of totalitarianism, as evidence of the state's power to punish through banishment. He refused to give a Proustian bow to nostalgia and saw childhood under totalitarianism as an old woman with "breasts dangling, her belly flapping / a helmet on her head." The past offers no consolation, no refuge from exile where one lives

> haggard and worn, without mercy or a vessel
> to gather your extremes and to give a field of quiet
> like the fall of a broken wing
> in the open palm of indecision.

Even when one succeeds in planting a human connection in the country of exile, other forces come into play to destroy this fragile achievement. "[I]n a second—my rose finds her kin," and the speaker is left asking again, *"Where to now?"* The details of the experience are sketchy precisely because exile is a narration that aborts any attempt at creating a narrative.

The Gulf War in 1991 awakened in Janabi's poetry an insurmountable sense of despair. Like many exiles from international pariah nations, he took a position that no one wanted to hear. Opposed to his government and banished from his country, he still could not affiliate himself with the powers that mercilessly pounded his homeland. The images that he saw televised from the war zone were of places he knew and of people whose faces resembled his own. Some political exiles can take their new places of refuge for granted and can shape lives based on the hope of return, but for Janabi the destruction of Iraq extinguished any hope of such a return. As the war began, Janabi's relations with his people in Iraq dissolved in a mass of destruction and destitution. The exile itself became a secondary thought for him and for his relatives because their suffering was overwhelming; they began to reside beyond his imagination, which rendered them virtually nonexistent. We see this feeling expressed in the poem "The Storm." The scene described in the poem is apocalyptic, which is the way the poet viewed the Gulf War. The survivors the speaker comes in contact with are all nonhuman—a snake flicking its tongue behind iron bars and stones running and tumbleweeds pleading, seeking refuge from the storm that is "guarded by metal insects and ferocious winged herds." The storm has depleted the land of people and memories of them, and even the most obdurate inhabitants of that rugged terrain are in danger. The Gulf War obliterated the past for Janabi and rendered it a wasteland.

While in Indiana, Janabi wrote a group of American poems. These are mostly represented in the last section of this book. In these poems, his poetry took a different turn. While he continued to explore the image and to operate cinematically, the poems he wrote in that period became shorter, and their tone was more observant and guarded. He approached the American scene carefully, limiting his observations to personal encounters and concerns rather than to larger political issues. Still, in poems such as "The Abyss," Janabi managed to address isolation and solitariness as especially American concerns. The image of watching a neighbor being attacked by a crocodile and the speaker's inability to save his neighbor attempt to rethink the American answers to questions of individual freedom and social engagement. The exile Janabi met his match, his opposite, in the United States, a nation of exiles, a people for whom, historically, individual liberty and its subsequent social disconnection is valued over solidarity. These American poems suggest that Janabi's poetry, while committed to its aesthetic choices of exploring the image and surrealism, can change and expand to negotiate challenging questions posed to it by new realities.

Unlike most translators who begin with a literal rendition and move toward a liberal one, I began translating these poems liberally and then tried to make them literal. I wanted to see what an English equivalent would sound like at first. In most cases I was doing this as I was reading the poems. Though my mother tongue is Arabic, my appreciation of a poem in Arabic does depend on how it would sound (in my head) in English. If, as I was translating freely, I found that the poem had an acceptable cadence in English, I went on to finish the translation.

To me, this process is similar to ballroom dancing. A translator's job is to provide a dancing partner for the original poem. The greatest pair of dancers in the world have to be great individually. The act of translation attempts to provide a matching partner, as dictated by the original, and to create the dance. At first, I wanted to see to what extent the translated poem was a good English poem. Then I proceeded to revise my draft, edging closer toward the literal to the point where the English could dance along with the original, step by step, syllable by syllable.

Based on this principle, the selections in this book are representative of what I could accomplish as a translator/choreographer. I had to ask myself repeatedly whether I was choosing poems that fully represent Janabi's poetry. I have tried to do this to the best of my ability here, and the poems in this volume represent what I felt could best be rendered into English and at the same time reflect the rest of Janabi's poetry.

While I was in Indiana, I had a chance to ask the eminent translator Clayton Eshleman about the criteria he used in choosing which poems to use from the work of a poet he liked. He replied that he did not translate individual poems, rather he translated books of poems. In some ways, this makes a translator's work easier, in that the poet has made those decisions. I had asked Professor Eshleman this question because I wanted ideas about how to construct a book of Janabi's poetry. His answer was interesting but not helpful because Janabi's poetry, written in Arabic, has only seen the light in book form through Polish translations—the selections based on another translator's judgment and ability. Not being in the midst of the Arabic literary scene, Janabi has yet to publish a full volume in Arabic even though hundreds of his poems have been published in magazines. Having no book to translate, I went about creating one.

The usual way of organizing a volume of selected poems is to proceed in some sort of chronological order. To begin with, this was not Janabi's wish and I agreed with him. The original arrangement of the poems he organized had no sections and included twenty-eight poems. After Janabi left the United States, I had a chance to translate some of his American poems and some older ones. I tried to include these in the original arrangement he gave me, but something about it was uneven. I decided to reorder the poems on my own. The first section, I felt, must include the poems in which Janabi presents his themes most dramatically. These are mostly the poems written in Poland and Algeria during or right after the completion of his doctorate in drama. It is to this intensive study of modern drama that I attribute the poems' highly dramatized utterances. I think also that the poems in the first section, some of which were the first ones I read, best represent Janabi's experimental style and uniqueness as a poet. In these he is willing to go out on a limb, to be hyperbolic or whimsically tender.

In the second section I put together the poems that can be best described as cosmological. There is a poem entitled "An Initial Description," one entitled "The Rule," and a series of prescriptive poems entitled "The Pickaxe of Childhood," "The Yellow Face of Hunger," et cetera. In these poems Janabi is mostly defining the world for himself, creating the type of imagery he would end up using later in his poetry. I ended the second section with "Playing the Skull," a poem in which many of these cosmological definitions culminate and create the dramatic voice to be found in the first section.

In the third section where the poems are quieter, shorter, more realistic, Janabi shows his versatility as a poet. The cadence of these poems is more tentative and less dramatic. They take place, mostly, in this world. "In Frost" is provoked by an instance in which the speaker is bending to tie his shoes. *"Willis Barnstone's Masks"* is addressed to a real person. "The Search for My Grandmother" is a dramatized elegy for the poet's grandmother. In these poems he comes closest to writing autobiographically. What excites me most about these poems is Janabi's ability to transform his surrealist technique from dramatic monologue into pure lyric. Here it is difficult to attribute these poems to "a speaker" because it is in this group that Janabi speaks as an individual.

While working on this volume I had an advantage rarely available to most translators. Janabi was practically my neighbor, and I met with him regularly to ask about particular words or phrases, and sometimes sentences I did not fully understand. In many cases I had a number of versions of the same poem, and I chose the version I liked best even though my choice did not always coincide with his. In a few cases, particularly in the newer poems, I suggested that some changes be made in the original Arabic. And in the same way that I chose the versions of poems that I liked, Janabi chose which of my suggestions to incorporate. All of this is to say that the project Janabi and I undertook involved all the aspects that come into play when a poet translates a living poet.

Translating a poem does not necessarily teach us about the creativity required to write poetry. It teaches us more about the creativity that is required for ethical conduct, about how to live in small spaces and how not to harm others. Translation also teaches us about deprivation and how to create beauty under extreme conditions. It is a uniquely human activity and a very civilizing one. And for that I am immensely indebted.

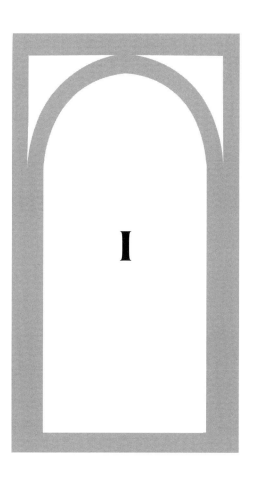

I

Incantation

Thank God for the two legs he gave me
and the bundle of ribs
and for my mien which he carved without favors or masks.
I crawl on two limbs or four
when the torturer hurls the steps of my tomorrow
and scatters my parts.
Thank God for forming me from clay and failure
and for placing in my soul a spark of the blazing fires of his love,
for telling me: be a chariot or a stone
                    be a rose or rain,
for telling me: be a Gehenna, Gehenna
in the tyrants' paradise,
for the first is life
and the latter is life.

A Window Small as a Palm, Vast as Suffering

From here to heaven, a shuttered window.
From here to exile, a wounded horse pulling another horse blessed by demons
    guarded by wasps.
From here to my brother dressed in evanescent white,
    to my mother's gray hairs dyed by the time to come
    with her son's coffin or the martyrs' parade,
    a thin hair

             of

                hope.
From here to border crossings, protecting their genitals with iron bars,
    a clearing
        for new quarrels and fresh kills.
From here to the Iraqi, in a pit below an abandoned window
    in the mud and trenches, in the dialogue between East and West
    in a dark storeroom
    in the cold with a whale gulping a ship
    in graves that beam with the light of their dead
    in darkening grayness
    in tombstones,
    a hoary merchant
    and a landlord awarding
    medals from his loot . . .

From here to my lungs
    I hear God howling at the edge of my blood,
    around him guards gripping clubs
    and a catapult dragged like a sin.
    In the space between my lungs

I listen for scraping and crackling
from an ancient age.
I see horses
kicking a man's chest.
And in front of me, wearing an iron skirt,
       a woman.
That's my wife, I say.
I have never seen her before.
A helmet on her head,
she places a rose
on my heart.
She weeps and is proud
of my death while murderers dance
waving posters of the guillotine.

From here to amusement parks
       to paralyzed grandchildren,
       foreign spies, and women from the East
       grinding saffron with the rubies of a corrupt kingdom
       with jasmine and chrysolites.
From here to canteens, to souls howling
       on a stone to delight the bellies of dreamy kings
       couched on the thrones of barren lands,
       with rituals
       and psalms chanted by harlequin poets and mercenaries—
       strangers, sacraments, elegies, ragged songs,
       mumblings, incense, and prayers—
       sacrifices appealing to God and the hanging rope.

From here to the sky, to a willow
to ringing chimes, to quince palms, to snow
       spilling tears in the valley—
       a window
              a window
                     wide as this pain.

Questions and Their Retinue

These are the questions and their retinue of poetry and prose.
There is no difference between one testicle and another except for
    swelling. Now I
        ask all
those who differentiate between a finger and another, a catastrophe
    and another,
a woman and another.
They give birth and were born on the banks of paralysis and weeping.
They have pointed hooves and before they emerge they kick the wombs
and the midwives' caves collapse. Afterward everywhere becomes a
    barren place.
They are born in a quilt that quickly turns into a street and a
    neighborhood,
a lavish yacht, an expansive harem, etc., etc.
Thank you. It was you, from the beginning, who forced us into writing
    verse, and
because the old meters
have calcified we now are trying a new form of expression
for the violets of failure, for the swings of despair,
for the crumbs of white tombs (white in wartime),
for the chirping of a Bedouin as he leans over a prostitute, soft and
    marble-like,
for the garbage heaps of plenty procreating
on foreign coasts,
always fleeing the holy books and their prohibitions.

This then is the bludgeon of civilization that forced us
to bring forbidden animals to till our lands,
pigs plowing our fields, grasshoppers in clinics,
grasshoppers slapping Alwasiti's* widow who gives birth

now (and forever) in a landfill-museum . . .
This is our heritage. Let us return to its chains and spears,
its freedoms and licentiousness.
What a marvelous indigenous cocktail fortified with prohibitions,
blessed by the computers of friendly allies!
Danke, Ça va, Good!

Once again we feel our bodies,
our fingers touching and listening attentively
for things, minerals, ores, and stones.
What a magical return to the stone ages! It is
the miracle of our offspring that we now bless with verses:

> As they plow our steps
> as they crack open the horizon
>   a grass blade of speech
> and Babylon weeping in refugee camps to a stone
> flung at us by witches,
> and our feet have yet to reach the Black Stone**
>   but the winds were generous
>   giving us an arm
> with which we struck the archipelago of the dark.
> Blackness smears fingernails
> with burns of light and a querulous wound.
> Naked we danced
> wiping off the dust of the night.
> To the river in the costume of willows
> we moved.
> (Fishermen began throwing clubs and dictionaries
> and heavy boots into the river
> and an idea began to glow.
> The naked ones screamed
> *Hang her! Hang her!*
> For centuries the ropes have been ready
> to be used in various ways.

In these arid, ravished cities
You, Ibn Munif, you must now write
the last chapter of your salt mine***
said a speaker with obvious contempt.
Everyone laughed then
and a child began hammering
the forehead of a poet
with a stone—the miracle of stone.
Now say what you will, the child said as though drunk.
Nothing except stone can subdue this metal.)

> . . . A flurry of stabs and behind the crooked statues
> a woman fell.
> (The poet said . . .)
> I said, *Lift your arms, body,*
> *and kiss her coat,*
> *her lacquered chest—*
> her knees were a violin
> her limbs reeds.
> And now she twists her fingers into a song
> released from the noose of stabs
> and proudly plants her nails in the dirt.
>
> These are the questions
> and their retinues are funerals that stretch from door to
>   door.
> These are the questions,
> stone and childhood,
> and the retinues are a herd of impoverished streets.
> A wide horizon.
> No window to shut us from it, no veil.

---

* Alwasiti's widow refers to a painting by Alwasiti titled "The Moment of Birth."
** The Black Stone is a holy stone in the Ka'aba shrine in Mecca.
*** A reference to novelist Abdulrahman Munif and his novel *Cities of Salt.*

Poems in a Manner of Speaking

I

I said to the word
Stay out in the cold
and it sat still.
I said to steps, *Open, spread*
and from my steps a herd began to stampede.
I said, *Wind, play your tune,*
branches, wake up!
What's behind is ruin.
What's ahead is dust.
I said, *Mother's voice, roll on the reeds of childhood,*
Father's time, broken in memory
like dew,
burst
burst!
and a voice reached me, crippled, crippled
like old age.
I said to lovers
The nights are yours and all that blooms.
I said to the day
You take the glitter
and to ash, *You take the flames,*
and for us in mourning, another mourning.
I said to possibilities, *Do all that can be done.*
I said, *Speech, boycott me.*
I said, *Word,*
spread your thighs
      and the word wept.

II

Said one crow to another
> *When trees fall or a storm gusts in,*
> *what will you do?*
> The crow preened its wings and flew.

Said the hemorrhage to the wounds
> *If the bleeding stops*
> *what will you do?*
> The wounds replied, *Then the healing will begin.*

Said fire to ash
and loggers to trees
> *If the rains pour, what to do?*
> Ash replied, *I and the trees*
> *will dance.*

Said one horse to another
> *What if we lose a bet one day?*
> *What will we do?*
> The other replied, *We will flee.*

Said the prophet to the god
> *At the end of creation, what did you do?*
> The god answered, *I rose to the sky and rested.*

Said the poor one to the loaf
> *If I come toward you,*
> *what will you do?*
> The loaf answered, *I will become dry and hard.*

And when the corpse said to Man
> *Beware*
> *of these herds*
> Man wrapped his head and slept.

III

A toast to satire.
A toast to eulogies.
A toast to women.
This is how the liquor of words is brewed,
and so let us begin with death,
a flower, an embryo the world searches for.
In its footprints prophets live.

Said the adulteress
When it comes that I have no man
to take refuge by my lips or a star to light my way,
I will leave at each doorstep
a path that leads to my heart's grief.

Said the storm
to clothes, to women's souls and planets,
to old maids and decrepit desire
I will color the branches and move,
taking with me all that was prohibited
by fatherhood and pride.

Said the mothers
We have in these naked branches
the fruits of desolation and wonder
and guards who stand watch at night
and who die of hunger to be born.

Said the soul to the body
A shoe
equals
my blood,
and my blood
is a dead

date palm.
Claim
for yourself
what remains within you
of the blood of love and wine and roses.
In a moment all men become dummies
and words turn to pebbles.
Claim for yourself
all that remains within you
of the waves' shiver and touch, whisper
and sway.

Said one soul to another, *Be*
my lampoon, my eulogy, the rose
of my ravished desert . . .
and to Babylon and miracles,
farewell, farewell.

Open Form

Song—
    If I were not a body
    if my words were not mixed with my despair-ridden sands
    if frenzied worms were not feeding on the nectar of this vicious
        wound
    I would have poked out the eyes of despair dozing among
        clouds of fumes.
                (O ravished days
                O moons gone mad.)
    If the stone falling from my ribs were not a slaughtered nation
    if the echoes were not a chorus of brays
    I would have shoved the spiders and snakes
    from this country that had its feathers plucked.
                (O torn limbs
                O invading herds.)
    If the date palm were bald
    if happiness on the hawk's beak were not crooked
    if every second did not have blackened lips
    I would have taken trees for clothes and rivers for beds
    and happiness a companion in this abysmal hiding place.
                (O axe carved
                in the body of a peacock
                the loggers have left
                and the axe now sinks.)
    If I were not a deserted body
    I would have pushed the spider and the snake
    from this exhausted land that had its feathers plucked.

The age of despair—
    A woman old and decadent
    hunched in her chair
    sucking on the loneliness of her hands
    begging for heaven's mercy,
    wet are her fingertips and eyes.

The kiss—
    Because it has no ring
    or hands or tongue,
    because it is a soft temptation
    incapable of shocking age, time, and place,
    welcome to its death.

A stone in the road—
    (Words hang from the poet's shoulder
    and the tongue rolls in narrow alleys
    searching for a realistic frame.)

Mud, candles, and other details—
    I wish silence were a woman
    and pythons were stones.
    I wish roads were kingdoms leading to the mist of safety.
    I was a princess in a crowd of luminous stars.
    I walk the alleys and hear my happiness and its mellow thrum.
    I fling the echoes at the deluge of the roads.
    There is no meaning to this night, no meaning
    to a thing either extinguished or lit
    gathering word-droppings in an abandoned bowl
    in a punctured
    breastless phrase.
    If only the desolate prairie
    would become music and a forest raging black,
    if only the bolted hearts
    would surrender to the body free-leaved and bare.

What is this prey and its carved limbs and cloven hooves
chased by marksmen, ghosts poking its eyes,
chased by raiding gangs and carts?
What is this song and its mummified limbs
in these cities of spiders and magicians, scandals and salt?

If only hopes are clearings where we can walk.

Poems without a Shelter

I

A circular night ended,

from east to west walking on four.
The south
a step
a step toward sunset.
The north
a tender-skinned child
a helmet on her head . . .

A night of steel ended
and the day is a diminishing star
and I run between night and a new day.

II

A Crusaders' night ended
and I invited melancholy and noise
    to a café,
    invited the day for a walk,
    the stars to a tavern on my street,
    to night and spies crouching on the road.
    Nothing in my hand but an Andalusian cup
        that broke.
    I cried, *Father,*
      what passed,
      will it return?

He shouted, *The past is an instant*
                    and an echo.
I cried, *No!*
                    Give me back my first cry.
He cried back
                    What passed will not return.
The road to fire is a burned sacrifice.
I cried, *O . . .*

Then dawn sieged us
memories,
I and the wooden bed
and the towering flower,
I
and a conscience made of gold.

III

A night ended
                    in descent.
Everything moved quickly
                              quickly.
The island streets
the voice of Babylon and wailing women
my mother's cloak
a camel's hump
a shiver of love
a bloody kiss
everything passed
                    quickly
                         quickly
                              in
                                   the glory of exodus.

To Where

1. Where steps are you taking this distance
        with a spiral of my blood
        and my mother's coat
        with my sister's solitude and my father's silence
        and a friend's collapse?
        Does my heart drop with the disillusion
        of date palms
        or with a miracle to sweep pavements and to chase
        demons with the fork in the road?

2. I see in the smashing of mirrors
        our childhood
        her old breasts dangling, her belly flapping
        a helmet on her head
        her hands
        two blazing flames.

3. Where are we heading to? Hoof of Thunder, marble feet
        spreading a blanket of hope
        passing with our rock solid loneliness.

4. I see what remains of my kin and friends, jewels made of dust.
        I see that the candles
        and the perfume bottles are buried in silt
        and that what we read of Laila's love and the devotion to
            the land
        are a mythical dream
        from a mutinous age.

5. Where to, my body? Muddied and raging in the prairie dust
   haggard and worn, without mercy or a vessel
   to gather your extremes and to give a field of quiet
   like the fall of a broken wing
   in the open palm of indecision.
   I say, *Where to, my body?*

6. I see myself beating at darkness
   tossing my heart's weeds
   at a tamed lion
   stretching my coat to cover
   the shameful parts of poetry and poets.

7. I saw a gang of grasshoppers
   and another scaled and gray
   waving for me to stop—
   commanding me—*Do not lose your Arab tongue*
   and when I stopped
    I saw
    I was without a country or guide,
   my blood spilled in corridors and in barbaric rooms.

8. To the rhythm of a woodpecker
   to the hissing of snakes
   in these jammed roads we walk
   I, the Bedouin, and the flower of my soul
   strolling gardens and alleyways
   and in a second—my rose finds her kin.
   And you my love, *Where to now?*

9. I see a scarlet dome
   blazing with light
  and I hear a low raspy voice
  coming with the wind.

None other than my love's voice.
I stroked my hair
and found a country and a double-edged axe wailing.
I found vineyards, a goblet, and two beasts
sipping my blood.
I said, *Drink up*
and pour the remains
on the bald head of this wretched age
with the blessing of God and the messengers

amen.

A Party

We came with crows and wheat
and when our munitions were depleted
we mixed wind-whispers and stares.
We came with the mourners yesterday
and when our eyes were gouged
we stood between the tides of whispers and confessions.
We came with lovers and singing
and when our hands withered
we walked a step in melody and another step.
We came with apples and grapes and women
and when euphoria broke us into dance
our hands became cups, our visions became companions.
We said we will shed all that passed with wine and sex
until darkness walked out stumbling drunk.
The women screamed at us
> Let us all go!
> All that remains in us of the sweetness of love and caressing
> is the ash of ecstasy and concealment.

We returned with crows and wind
and when our shirts tattered, we tore them off
to run wild in the clothes of night and trees.
An embryo, virginal and repleated
in the feast of devils and storms.

Savage Continents

In these forests, in their embroidered dresses
> or black bones
> someone knows how they begin and end.
> Someone knows how to move without stumbling
> in search of the soul's guiding flame,
> someone who weeps genuinely
> and someone who pretends to weep,
> someone who cries, *O Fire, O Gilded Wedding*
> *be my flag and draw my steps.*
> A darkness
> has shamelessly crowned himself a king.

In these swamps
> I saw them like worms enter.
> How they knelt to him, how they twirled around him.
> I left my filly
> unbridled
> mad, galloping on the prairie.
> Someone was crying, *O prairie, prairie-e-e-e*
> > nothing except an echo.
> I saw the filly of the Euphrates
> crazed and galloping on the prairie.

I followed her
> and my cape ballooned
> with wind and dust.
> When I asked them for the way
> my cape filled with grass and stones
> and when I said, *Let us go*
> my cape ripped to pieces and I cried, *O prairie,*
> *cinders and dust are my clothes.*
> I hung my heart on an olive tree

and in the Baghdad of my allegiance
and the peninsula of my heart
tossing and turning like a holy verse.
No color here, blackness is white and whiteness black.
These cogwheels are our gold
and the singer's nectar.
The wailers died
and everyone has taken to song.
I followed them with black and white
with green and red, with sound and echo
with a nation of women
naked and grieving.
I said, *Let this be Sheba.*
Is there any word?
Is there a word?
Baghdad, Baghdad
the hoopoe has burned
and all are like prey
in a race with the wind.
I cried, *O prairie*
my heart hangs from an olive tree,
O prairie-e-e-e.
I followed them with a nation of women, naked,
their hair ruffled and coarse.
I cried, *These steel wheels are our gold.*
When we arrived
waters flowed red, red
and the roads were empty
except for smoke and burned skeletons.
There were no signs
because this is a day of doom.
Ash was the only gold.
I followed her with red and white
white and red, sound and echo

          and I saw my filly
wrapped in blood
mad, galloping on the prairie.
I cried, *O prairie*
nothing but an echo
O prairie-e-e-e.

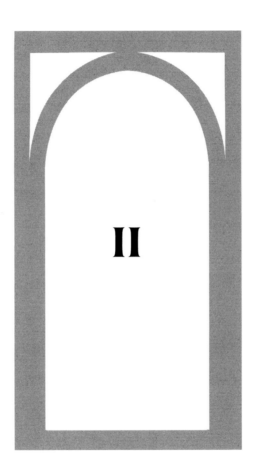

II

An Initial Description

I will not pass by its sitting rooms tattooed with sighs,
its dusty walls—
how they used to spy on me!
I will not pass by its desperate garden
where I was chased by one obsessed
with abusing young poets.
I will not pass by its women
wrapped in the blackness of eternity
and the uncertainty of night,
where longing stares from robes,
the open slits
saying, *You may only look.*
I will not pass by the corridors,
the slopes bent like turtle backs.
(I stand now stripped of all that I inherit.)
I will not pass by the dead who fence it in.
I see them groping at the coattails
of the passersby, pleading for mercy.
I will not pass by its single gate,
single square, the shrine of its single imam,
and its single cemetery, edges gilded with sand,
calm as a cat surrounded by a brigade of dogs!
I doubt that I will pass by it,
where coffins lick the houses' ribs,
where the last clue was swept by a storm.
I doubt that I will pass by it,
and if I do, I must, like that ancient poet,
hold my will in my right hand.

Poems of the New Regions

1) House Songs

What do you call a stone that now refuses to fall?
What do you call a stone that eats itself,
that withers in the light of a candelabra,
           that falls in love at the whim of the wind?
What do you call a stone ground by wind
        in a shattered pot,
        a room where tenants pay their debts,
        where children write their lessons
        under a porthole that lets in flashes of lightning?
        What do you call the miracle of lightning?

The solitary date palm
in the house yard,
      the solitary room
      and a forest of eyes,
the body hanging
      from the wall.
What do you call a stone rejected by a wall?
The solitary date palm
reveals its chest, and leans gently
      to a stubborn girl.
What do you call a stubborn girl?
        What do you call a stone scratching itself
        that withers in the light of a candelabra,
        that falls in love at the whim of the wind?

2) Petroleum Valley

In dark nights
branches hold the mystery of words;
branches drowse at night, an hour,
                        then scream.

In dark nights
every bird is a predator, every evening a black wave,
                        an infinite sea
                        and closed eyes.

On gloomy nights
only one nation knows the secret of the valleys,
a nation washing its hands in oil
forming from the shape of the plain, daylight and trees.

3) Picture of a Hand

White hand
                black hand
                                black white hand
and a face fixed on a rose where days bloom,
                where seasons come to a close.
A hand flows calmly
on a field fleeing through cracks of light
and paints everything with the color of eyes.
A hand tattoos the earth's rug with leaves
and surrenders to a wave of boughs.

4) A Child

In the distant ocean, the sky migrates to the sea
        exhausted, pummeled by the world
        like a summer cloud.

In the distant ocean, the sky lays on the surface of the sea,
        a chain
        of jagged edges hung
        among the hues of the hills—
        the wide plains behind the ocean's edge.
In the wide sky, a misty bird,
in the obstinate ocean, an Arab child.

5) The Wisdom of the Coasts

A wave stretches slowly
        wrapping its waist with shellfish
        and rages furiously
        breaking shells and borders, revealing mysteries.
A wave, an ancient proverb,
        a butterfly asleep on a bed of flowers.
A wave, the spirit of a ship punctured by the surge.
A wave, the head of a horseman exhausted from spinning
who rested his head on the water's rug.
        A wave, a dead horseman's head.

The Pickaxe of Childhood

Piercing your stone ribs
>your skin now embroidered with neon
>your imaginary sun
>piercing to you,
>to the garbage dumps of the universe
>and the blazing tear.

In the name of roads and gravel
in the name of shattered poems
in the name of branches and detention camps
I blow in a horn
in black stones and white, in plains and mountains.
>I cry to everyone
>*O Continents, O Winds,*
>>*O Waves,*
>>*O Prairie-e-e-e.*

The earth splits.
>Night and day run toward me.

I blow in water, and deserts come
to me like a forest of virgins.
We crawl like ants, like winds and rain
like the speed of light.
We split that body
with the pickaxe of childhood,
searching in your flat breasts
for a drop of silver
and a new flag
for the body newly born.

The Yellow Face of Hunger

Take a piece of paper
take a pen
take a stone
take all you wish
and leave one thing.
     Beware not to touch a chair.
     Beware not to stir the air
     for it starves in poems.
     Take a piece of paper
     take a pen
     draw a cigarette on a chair
     a boat and a picture of a wretched ferocious childhood.

Take the old melancholy
leave us the poems of bread.
Take your body
leave us the legacy of date palms, a prison, and a healthy conscience.
     Take a rock
     and an old picture.
     Try now to write the eyes
     after their ink dries.
     There is a square.
     Leave the new stone near the woman and the flowers.
     In a moment a date palm will shoot through the earth
     and jails will shut down.

Taxes remain
old clothes remain
stone benches remain

empty, empty
except for dust and scattered joys.
>Take a defeated hero
>take a poor man
>give him a loaf of bread.
>He will write poems and make bread.

Poems remain
the new theaters remain
joys remain
empty, empty
except for noise and passages endlessly repeated.
>Take a piece of paper
>take a pen
>and draw a chair, a lover, and a boat.

Heart of the Night

The fingertips of memory
or the silver eyelashes of fatigue,
hyacinth clothes
or the rings of a ravished marriage,
cogwheels on my brow.

The scream of the sunset
or the shiver of leaves
surprised by a cloud.
The femininity of the valleys as they burst forth
or the cough of a fat history.

The catastrophe will occur
thus spoke that soothsayer of words.
The catastrophe
has the growl of mist
and the teeth of time
jagged like desperate contempt,
discarded and rough like me.

With my tottering heritage
and my bloating despair
I call you—
angel of the heights above—
wait for me.
I am the one drowning
in others' sins.

This stubborn prairie
is our only consolation,
where panthers stagger
and things burn
because all is firewood,
and I burn
for my want of you.

The birds winged with stone
the stone with the head of a bird
the meadow that throbs like a falcon
the mountain with the eyes of a hawk
our endless, benevolent space
and the lost traces of harmony—
this is our gushing music
singeing the last heart of the night.

The Claws of Memory

Stretch out nights
wide as desolation in ruins.
Break out days
your pubescent wars
in the mud of exile.
Nothing remains in the wall
except the claws of memory
and the shadows of elderly buses
as they point to the body tossed at the stations
to turn around
where there are mountain goats and pears
and chimneys smoking in the valleys
where the songs of the tribes
sting
the heart
of stone.

The Chemistry of Knowledge

For us a stone swallowed by the sea
the grass on whose breasts the dust walks
a cloud the suns have drunk up
and books destroyed on their way to the printer.
For us strange words
                and names from the age of A'ad.
For us cities without streets or balconies.
For us men with ten eyes
                who wear a thousand shirts and neckties
                who have a thousand genitalia.
For us men with ten eyes and heads made of stone.
For us a wine that renders the bull drunk, and clouds and wind and
night
                and demons and poetry.
For us a wine that intoxicates God and makes him weep
                but that does not touch our presidents at all.
For us shrines
                wide as two earths.
For us a country wretched, wretched
                groveling in ash.

The Rule

The rule is
(you come naked, no declarations, no questions)
your steps deliberate and slow
your body wrapped
with a rag
a leaf.
The rule is
you mumble or scream
say Yes
then No
like this, alternating, until speech begins to spin.
The rule is
(you leave naked, candles and prayers brushing against you).
The rule is
you are now a winged memory,
you are the rule.

Playing the Skull

I may spread my sobs on my skin.
I may draw on the sand
      a tomb bearing the soul's address.
Tonight I collect my suspicions in a bottle,
I scatter myself on the sidewalks of love
and play the music of the dead.
      Tonight I flog my love
      and burn my passions the following day
      with stars, clouds, and wind.
      In the shirts of the earth
      my dreams were a circle,
      red chains and white.
      God was a loaf of bread I chased
      in the morning
      and in secret I fixed my eyes the devil's way
      and learned of the wine of desire and the rains that pour
                             like torrents
      learned of the poverty that flows in torrents.
The hung trees told me and torrents warned me
in a moment a spear will grow out of my limbs,
a spear leaved with miracle-dreams and skeletons
      and a weeping woman
      and a laughing woman.
O woman who has nothing but wind and clothes
      I long for the nerves of the universe to crack,
      I long to bury my face in a greater rage.
      Time teaches us that patience weeps,
      that there are no leaves within us, no excess.
      Each huddles by the window of his miseries and weeps.

For the earth is made of skulls—the best ones emerge
to play their music, to dance and fall.
When did fear become a loaf of bread, and love a sky?
I will flee my skull,
I will draw imaginary steps between the dead and the living,
I will hang my skull from children's belts.
I dream of a throne, love.
                              I rehearse my death every minute,
I, the nihilist who falls like a needle
                              in the sand.
A prickly shrub grows out of my bed, a tree and a cause.

We were two
the wall and I.
We hungered and the wall wound around me.
Tourists left, and my lover left
and a wall wound around me and left.
Who thought that a wall could walk?
The wall was white,
the wall became red,
the wall became black,
the wall fell.
I crossed to the other bank
and I knew that I was the beginning.

The Pharaoh's army passes by my head.
At times it camps by my feet
          and at times it moves on.
The world offers me poison to drink and I refuse
          offers me poison and I refuse.
          The world like the Pharaoh's army
          moves quickly and brings me the dead
          and passes by my ears,
          sprays poison on my skin and moves on.

The world has become skin and the murdered an army.
      The world was like an apple,
      I know the world was like an apple
      but the dead do not eat.
The Pharaoh's army (a friend).
A world like an army is killing me
and is spraying poison on my heart.
The poisoned skin falls off me and the poisoned head.
      I say the Pharaoh's army is a friend
      (the Pharaoh is my love).
      The world is abandoned and the dead have drowned
      and the world like an apple is coming toward you
      so take my heart for a plate.
      But the dead do not eat.
      The Pharaoh's army passes quickly.
      Drink your wine by the dead.
      The world is abandoned and the dead ones have drowned.
      All the grasses embrace a skull to wear one
      and the farmers and workers are testaments
      that the grass reads and the Nile searches for
      in the Pharaoh's head
      in the year of the elephant.
      The Nile searches for its dead, and the earth searches,
      and the dead are an army.
      Like a drunk's head—this world, this age.
      Do not despair.
      Take my heart and read the names of the dead.
The world runs in my head like a spear
I vomit, I squeeze my head
I cross toward death
I gather people and they cry.
      This mad one is a raging fire. Move away!
We comfort the shocked ones with patience. The defeated ones
we comfort with patience.
Lovers, laborers, farmers, beggars, we comfort with patience.

Who will build a chair
legs made of arteries
ribs for wood, teeth for nails
for this hardhearted country
to rest in during its comatose hours?
Who will build a hearse
for this hardhearted country
to spend its old age in?
Here I am, my country, like a corpse with my head severed.
I vomit my people, I rise in them like water
I cover the earth, I flood.
Here I am, my country, like a cloud raining patience
raining longing and tenderness.
Like hopelessness I blaze,
the porcelain of my eyes and my skull are despair.

Rain you say, and I rain
and I am befriended by streams.
Rain and I rain
and I am befriended by fear.
Rain and I rain
and I am befriended by destitution.
Rain and I rain
and I am befriended by tears—
only a lover knows my secret.

III

Qassidas

Affection

From her waves I had a crown that covered my lungs.
I could have poured a little of my soul or much.
I could have tightened my lips
to gather pure honey from the sea—Isabel.
The crown fell to the chasm of affection.
Alone, seashells sang on the coast.

     Froth

          now fills

               the lovers' hearts.

Solitude

(I could have chosen the wind
after I was chased
by the armies of eternity
after the horns of solitude
blared in my body
after my poet friends
[they and the dreamy revolutionaries]
were used up.

O the chirping of solitude
when a man in the epitome of his annihilation
stares at her quarreling breasts!)

Birds

(I could have chosen the wind,
could have moved ahead
running around bends and in the prairie
bareheaded as usual,
propelled by the cap of hope
not the cloak of dispersion
or the bracelets of memory,
carrying the soul and the word.

Birds stared contemptuously
as tigers gnawed a chunk of the wild.)

Joy

(O my wretched Glory
you could have been useful to me
once and forever

with the rustle of joy.

When joy is ecstatic
her hands no longer fill up with fog,
her lips are not as distant as clouds,
her sun is no longer a dried, peeled apple
and my cry to her does not boom and swell
like an autumn tear.)

Sea Songs

The first forest released me
to a tumultuous morning.
The wind gathered my steps
and snow became a pyramid glistening
in the bottom of the night.
Ravenous songs wailed from the sea
This is the eye of the flame.
I watched and life appeared to me
as a diamond in her hand.

Stars were wrapped
in her dress and earrings and perfume.
She took them off in the gusting wind
and they were unraveled by the sea.

Hope

I could have chosen lightning,
could have moved
ahead
shining an old dusty beauty,
searching
in this mercurial archipelago
for hope.

Moroccan Diary

Saturday

I am howling in the prairie of the Casbah.
My voice is ash and the day is a dirt pit.

Sunday

Bonjour Madame,
Bonjour Monsieur . . .
Silence and memory,
then the talk ends.

Monday

Friends, we are from the tribes of earthworms
and hippopotami crawling in space,
flying in drowsiness
without wings
or clothes.

Tuesday

The shops puffed up their cheeks,
their innards and their mouths,
poets braying inside them,
journalists sweeping words,
waiting for the death of a new poet.

Friday

I see, friend, that you are squeezing
grapes in other cities
lost in the haze of colonnades
where the hours you spew from your eye sockets
wrap around your neck
a rip-saw of memory
accustomed to confiding in you.

Paradises, Soldiers, and Stags

I am content with bitter words,
 with a fluttering spike of wheat.
  I am content with broken branches;
   I say someday this wooden space will disappear.
    Sometimes I am content with soup, and with the water of grapes.
     I am content with the hope that the echo of a storm
      will swing between me and peace.
     I am content with the chirpings of the dark.
      I say soon, soon they will come
       to wash my face with dregs of dew.
        I am content with faucets and afterthoughts,
         with the stones that cover autumn's bare back,
          with a snake flicking its tongue behind my ribs. I say
           maybe the loved one will come
            to me in a dream and she arrives.
             I am content with the gushing of seasons, the stutters of
              memory,
             with the dazzle of stars, the flutter of a feeble heart, with
              whispering and caressing and dance,
             with him who does not achieve his mischief.
            I am content and I brag about the wings of a crow,
             something to bless my steps
             and to heap on my grief a mountain of dirt.
            I am content with the talk of rebel boys, sayings
            of lunatics, soothsayers, and the prophet-like poor.
            I am content with the one who does not reach his desolation.
           (They stretch out to the flow of his shock.)
           I am content with paradises in their cradles,
          with stags lisping flames,
         cunning soldiers shrinking
        without leniency
        and a creaking past.

I am content with dew as a bird stings the pistil where it lay.
I am content when a dream pricks my night with its beak
 or reveals that the beginning will be a further strain
  and that winter is the whistling of stones.
    I am content with my grandmother's cane, the courtyard, a pot of tea,
      a jug of water,
    my mother's cloak, my neighbor's prayer beads, and the palm
      fronds hidden in the victim's rib cage.
  I am content with the little that is much,
 but in the end I will accept nothing less
than to clutch the impossible's throat.

The Storm

The woodpeckers were pecking at my head, and I was tormenting myself. I grabbed a handful of dust, and it escaped. There were the scars of a waterwheel, traces of pasture, and on the streambeds the shadows of gazelles, a snake flicking its tongue behind bars, reminding me of my grandmother's tomb. She wanted it to be made of hay and palm fronds. The woodpeckers were biting space, contemptuously scattered, pinning me in place.

Are the woodpeckers warning me?

The wind plays its music, steps disperse, the mountain quails fling themselves in space, and I see a stone running, tumbleweeds pleading with the saved for help, sun strings disappearing behind black stars. There is dusk now scratching wings; there is a storm guarded by metal insects and ferocious winged herds.

The woodpeckers are strewn on the ground, and I am pecking at myself. I hold the grains of life and they seep from my hands.

The Abyss

A crocodile caught my only neighbor
in a distant village—
I was once a spectator, once a survivor.

I did not want to seem indecisive or afraid,
I did not want to be left alone,
I stretched out my hand hoping to save him.
I was the only rescuer in this distant village.
I was struck on the forehead,
the crocodile was lashing at my forehead.
I was not a hero when I retreated
caught with the outstretched
limbs
of despair.
I became a spectator, that's all.
I saw from a hill the crocodile
crack the head of my only neighbor.
I saw him crushed in the dark tunnel
crushed in a jagged world.
I was looking from above at the dark jungle
with the eyes of bloated despair
with the eyes of my only neighbor
where I was the only rescuer.

The Sail

Nothing but memories
    slithering angrily
    sometimes sustaining me
    sometimes gnawing at my forehead and my clothes.
Nothing but the tongue
    of a mocking rabbit in the wild.
Nothing but squirrels
    sauntering between
    a branch and a girl's dress.
Nothing but brave animals.
Nothing but the music of nakedness.
(My father was swept by the storm
and my brother disappeared returning
from the war of nights
and a few friends
were ripped to tatters
on the road to life.)
Nothing but the arrow of whispering and motion
rushing, rushing
toward the sail of the storm.

Autumn

To this evening, the taste of old age;
to old age, the voice of dimmed manhood.
To the country that broke my boat,
to the country that tore my body
                    then betrayed my passions,
to that country, the taste of old ash.

To the wind, the whinnying of raped women;
to the houses
                    when they begin their procession
                    in the body's dust,
                    a choir of toads
                    and naked singers.

Where is my holy drum,
where is my iron stride
in this revived autumn?

In Frost

I knelt to tie my shoes in the frost
and heard the rattle of an Indian's throat
or maybe the groan of an animal led to slaughter.
I imagined men bearing their weapons—extinct
before the Fifth Amendment of the Bill of Rights was recited,
since all applauded it and drank a toast to dynamite
as a charm against evils.
I could not control myself. I kicked off my shoes,
danced and danced with the lightness
of one returning to heaven,
until my feet swelled.
And as I felt the bed for the remains of memory,
the memory of forests, meadows, pavements and streets,
the memory of mountain goats and eagles and dinosaurs
pleading with me
to give storms the leap of motion,
to give horses the calm sleep
of a veteran of a war of beasts.
And as I felt the bed
for the remains of the pain of memory,
I saw one of the extinct men—
deep-set eyes and a torch behind him—
point his weapon at me.

The New World

On New World Street, in its usual labor pains, where vigilant lenses observe naked truths, where the cameras of the day have no time for reflection, I saw door handles shaped like lions and shut doors staring from the balcony of the old world. I touched them with the lightness of a shy expert, and when I stared at the hidden reliefs, I found, carved in bronze, the names of lovers who died defending the city and, in another corner, names of authors and artists who passed away long ago. On New World Street I sipped coffee and watched two lovers whisper to each other, and from the end of a hall crowded with expressionist paintings, a famous local song blared.

Willis Barnstone's Masks

I do not care for the solitude of fingers
as they beckon from pleasure's bed.
I do not care for the plenitude of justice
where creatures race toward their demise
or for the sweetness of a dream
where the tongue is a dangling bitterness.
I do not care for the drawn fist of courage
or for the whimpers of animals drowning in the mud of hope.
I am not concerned with meadows crowded with the tents
of those who survived the sultans' false epics.
I am not concerned with leaves
and their difficult breathing every fall.
I am not concerned with the sea's ecstasy, the overflow
of froth whenever the bottom fills.
I am not concerned with this observant blind man, Borges,
and his cane fluttering like an angel
or the monastic climate of the Cultural Revolution.
How many misdeeds have we poets committed?
How many mistakes?
I am not concerned with that fly caught between a spider's jaws.
I am not concerned with that climate.

What I do not really know, Mr. Barnstone,
is the euphoria of childhood,
the burning log of youth.
What I do not know, my friend,
as you caress the fur of your scalp
(nostalgically) whispering a few words—
what I do not know are those masks on the wall
as they cling to the axe of time.

The Search for My Grandmother

In this courtyard
feathers and fingers of gold,
the cane
her hair, her wooden wedding comb
and that pitcher silent and blue.
A kingdom of dust.
I shake it off
and it returns like drizzle.
I see her:
She gasps
staggers forward
staggers back
and explodes with tears.
I whisper: Grandmother.
I scream: Grandmother!
I repeat, I rave
and suddenly
she vanishes in smoke.

For Hope All the Eyes in the World

Each pretends in his own way:
the liar that he is truthful
and the truthful one that he shuns lies.

&

The sharp knife cuts
fearing it will rust.

&

The longest journey is the word's
between mind and tongue,
and the shortest journey
is that between heart and lip.

&

You see me with your eyes
and I see you with my soul
and all we see is nought.

&

Things burn
because all is fuel
and I burn for my want of you.

&

Only one thing
distinguishes childhood from old age;
in the first we begin
and in the second we end.

&

A real word is wingless,
yet it soars high.

&

Exile and loss of memory
are two faithful partners,
but you must make them fight to death.

❧

Narrow thoughts
are like tight shoes.
If they do not stretch with use
abandon them.

❧

There is no meadow
for he who has no heights.

❧

Defeat has two eyes
and despair has three
and for hope all the eyes in the world.

❧

I beat my chest, I beat
hoping it will expand.

❧

Ideas are a primordial nakedness
and words must cover them.

❧

I washed my clothes
clipped my fingernails and left.
But I returned in a hurry
because I forgot to comb my thoughts.

Diary of an Angel

I

An angel is eternal. Clouds fall from his feet.
His sigh magnetizes the sea.
The bite of his lips, a universe teeming with mercy.
He contemplates his past gazing at the heavens.
With the light of his wings, with rising clouds of dust,
he fills all the dormant seashells—
an angel in dust, a fleeing phantom of gold.
I see murdered tribes and princes groveling
        in jungles and valleys.
I see tyrants panting behind him
and leprous servants carrying their masters' bellies.
I see wings turned to ash,
plains and herds drenched in outbursts of light.
I see a boulder guarded by an ancient glory.
On the beach—an angel is on the beach
contemplating from above how darkness pummels light,
how he burns and his shadow remains.

II

It was twilight in fog.
It was night and its shaking harbors
where desires dream,
where hopes stagger under the weight of delusions.
It was twilight
when I saw steam spirals swirl
and bodies whisper.

I cried   *America!*
            How ya' doin'?
Fine.
The godhead . . .
women with meteors falling from misty depths.
It was twilight.
It was a night surrounded by loyal friends.

III

As you embrace my scattered feathers
as you dance around the ashes of sins
glad, hopeful, and singing
write the last day
with the pen of bygone youth.
Paint the last day
with the ink of blood.

I envy you all
as you pack your memories
like a scattered herd
at the end of the world.

The Little Prince

The earth was portioned like this,
    in your size . . .
Water runs toward the crystal body
    and your small earth
    turns like blood.
Beware not to leave the garden,
    for around you there is tumult and ruin.
    Around you childhood
    sleeps in the dirt.
Beware not to point at anything
    even with severed fingers.
Beware not to write poems
  they will kill the tranquility in your heart,
  they will toss thunder at you and grief.

The earth was portioned like this,
    with the beat of your golden heart
and winds
  thunder
    and rain
circling in your unknown sphere
  spinning
in search of a drop of flame.

About the Author

Hatif Janabi was born in Iraq. Since 1976 he has lived as an exile in Poland and has published five bilingual volumes of poetry. He has won numerous poetry prizes in Poland and earned a Ph.D. in drama from Warsaw University where he now teaches Arabic literature and world drama. His poems, essays, and translations have appeared in many Arab literary magazines. Translations of his poetry have appeared in *International Quarterly, Indiana Review, Artful Dodge, Kaleidoscope, Connecticut Review, Graham House Review, Tampa Review, Breeze,* and *The Literatures of Africa and Asia.*

About the Translator

Khaled Mattawa is the author of *Isma'ilia Eclipse,* published by The Sheep Meadow Press in 1995. His poems have appeared in *Poetry, The Kenyon Review, New England Review, Callaloo, Crazyhorse,* and *The Pushcart Prizes XIX* (1994–95). An assistant professor of English and creative writing at California State University, Northridge, he was awarded the Alfred Hodder Fellowship at Princeton University for 1995 and 1996.